Mous

Crocodile

by Anna Halloran
illustrated by Mircea Catusanu

HOUGHTON MIFFLIN HARCOURT
School Publishers

Printed in China

ISBN-13: 978-0-547-02419-6
ISBN-10: 0-547-02419-3

15 16 17 18 0940 19 18 17 16
4500569761

Mouse lived by the river. He was very clever. He had a nice home with plenty of food to eat. There didn't seem to be anything more in life that he could possibly want.

Then, one day, Mouse looked across the water. Beside the village on the other side, he saw trees full of tasty fruit. Mouse was quite interested in the fruit on the opposite riverbank. He leaned over the water to get a closer look.

Snap! Crocodile had sprung from the water and snapped his teeth at Mouse. Mouse jumped back, startled.

Now here was a problem. Mouse wanted to get the fruit across the river. But Mouse knew that the minute he stepped into the water, Crocodile would eat him up!

Mouse thought, "How can I get that fruit when Crocodile lives in the river? I know I can outsmart Crocodile. I must come up with just the right plan."

Mouse began to search for a way to cross the river, but he couldn't find anything that would work. He thought and thought, and then he came up with the perfect plan!

The next day, Mouse went down to the river. It was time to put his plan into action. He called out, "Crocodile!"

Crocodile thought it was odd that Mouse was calling him. But he stuck his head out of the water just the same.

"What do you want, Mouse?" asked Crocodile. "Have you come to be my breakfast?"

Mouse answered, "Not at all. I have an important assignment from the King."

"The King!" exclaimed Crocodile. "What is the assignment?"

"The King is having a feast. He is inviting the crocodiles. He wants me to count all the crocodiles in the river. Then he will know how much food to provide," said Mouse.

"How can I help?" asked Crocodile.

"Please ask all the crocodiles to line up from this side of the river to the other. Then I will be able to count all of you," said Mouse.

The river <mark>contained</mark> many crocodiles. Crocodile dove into the water. He gathered all his family and friends. The crocodiles <mark>tossed</mark> and turned in the water. They got in position from head to tail. They made a line from one side of the river to the other.

9

"Perfect!" exclaimed Mouse. "I'm <mark>grateful</mark> for all your help, but before I begin, you must promise me one thing." He paused and looked each one of the crocodiles in the eyes.

"What is that?" the crocodiles asked.

"You must not eat me while I am counting. For if you do, I will not be able to report to the King," Mouse replied.

"Of course we will not eat you," promised the crocodiles. They were thinking of the King's feast and nothing else.

Mouse jumped on top of Crocodile's head. He counted, "One." He continued jumping on crocodiles and counting. At last, he reached the other side of the river and glanced quickly at the delicious fruit trees.

Crocodile was curious. "How many crocodiles are there? What will you report to the King?"

Mouse smiled. He answered, "There are just enough crocodiles to get me across the river. As for my report to the King, I will tell him that Mouse can outsmart Crocodile any day!"

With that, Mouse ran off to enjoy the fruit in the trees beside the village. All the crocodiles grumbled, but they knew that clever Mouse had tricked them once again.

Responding

TARGET SKILL **Understanding Characters** Think about the characters of Mouse and Crocodile in the story. Copy and complete the chart below.

Character	Action	What It Means
Mouse	He tells crocodile there will be a feast	Mouse knows what crocodile wants
?	?	?

Write About It

Text to Text Think about another story in which a character plays a trick. Is it right to trick someone? Write a paragraph about the trick and give your opinion. Include examples that tell more about your opinion.

✔ **TARGET SKILL** **Understanding Characters** Tell more about the characters.

✔ **TARGET STRATEGY** **Summarize** Stop to tell important events as you read.

GENRE A **folktale** is a story that is often told by people of a country.